MW00489821

Advent
Meditations
With
Fulton J. Sheen

Liguori

ONE LIGUORI DRIVE
LIGUORI MO 63057-9999

Imprimi Potest:
Thomas D. Picton, C.Ss.R.
Provincial, Denver Province
The Redemptorists

ISBN 978-0-7648-1658-1
© 2007, Liguori Publications
Printed in the United States of America
07 08 09 10 11   5 4 3 2 1

All rights reserved. No part of this pamphlet may be reproduced, stored in a retrieval system, or transmitted without the written permission of Liguori Publications.

Scripture quotations are from the *New Revised Standard Version of the Bible,* © 1989 by the Division of Christian Education of the National Council of Churches of Christ in the USA. Used with permission. All rights reserved.

Liguori Publications, a nonprofit corporation, is an apostolate of the Redemptorists. To learn more about the Redemptorists, visit Redemptorists.com.

To order, call 1-800-325-9521
www.liguori.org

Introduction

The word *adventus* is Latin for "a coming" or "an arrival." Advent is a season of joy as we prepare to celebrate Jesus' birth in Bethlehem. Advent is also a time to rekindle hope. Because God has entered our physical world, nothing in our human experience is beyond hope or meaning.

The quotations in this pamphlet, collected from the writings of Bishop Fulton J. Sheen, invite us to enter into the season of Advent as active participants, keeping in mind that "each single response to grace is a step taken toward peace and joy for all" (*Lift Up Your Heart*).

In *Seven Words of Jesus and Mary*, Bishop Sheen advised, "If you have never before prayed [with] Mary, do so now. Can you not see that if Christ himself willed to be physically formed in her for nine months and then spiritually formed by her for thirty years, it is to her that we must go to learn how to have Christ formed in us?"

With Bishop Sheen as our guide and the Blessed Mother at our side, may we make our hearts a tabernacle for the Savior of the world.

Sunday
First Week of Advent

Let Christ Be Formed in You

As God was physically formed in Mary, so he wills to be spiritually formed in you. If you knew he was seeing through your eyes, you would see in everyone a child of God. If you knew that he worked through your hands, they would bless all the day through....If you knew that he wants to use your mind, your will, your fingers, and your heart, how different you would be. If half the world did this, there would be no war!

HOW TO FIND CHRISTMAS PEACE

*The Mighty One has done
great things for me,
and holy is his name.*

LUKE 1:49

Monday
First Week of Advent

God's Whisper

God does not come in the thunder, but in the April breeze. Because he does not shout but only whispers, the soul must be careful not to neglect the visitation....To the eyes of faith, only two classes of people exist: those who say yes to God and those who say no to him.

LIFT UP YOUR HEART

Mary said, "Here am I,
the servant of the Lord;
let it be with me
according to your word."

LUKE 1:38

Tuesday
First Week of Advent

Our Response

God, who wishes to dwell in us, can always be evicted by a single word of dismissal. And so it is important to consider the way to respond to God's visitation—which we cannot prevent, but can cut short. The first necessity of our cooperation with God is the consciousness that it is he who is present; the will to know him causes our recognition of his presence. If we lack this readiness to know him, we are like those who smell and perceive no fragrance, taste and know no sweetness, touch and enjoy no ecstasy.

LIFT UP YOUR HEART

*"The Spirit of the Lord is upon me,
because he has anointed me to
bring good news to the poor."*

LUKE 4:18

Wednesday
First Week of Advent

God of the Second Chance

Though time is too precious to waste, it must never be thought that what was lost is irretrievable. Once the Divine is introduced, then comes the opportunity to make up for losses. God is the God of the second chance.... Being "born again" means that all that went before is not held against us.

PEACE OF SOUL

*May he so strengthen your hearts in holiness
that you may be blameless
before our God and Father
at the coming of our Lord Jesus
with all his saints.*

1 THESSALONIANS 3:13

Thursday
First Week of Advent

Communion With the Creator

There is a moment in every good meditation when the God-life enters our life and another moment when our life enters the God-life. These events transform us utterly. Sick, nervous, fearful individuals are made well by this communion of creature with Creator, this letting of God into the soul.

LIFT UP YOUR HEART

[God] has made known to us
the mystery of his will...
as a plan for the fullness of time,
to gather up all things in him,
things in heaven and things on earth.

EPHESIANS 1:9–10

Friday
First Week of Advent

God Comes to You

God walks into your soul with silent step. God comes to you more than you go to him. Never will his coming be what you expect, and yet never will it disappoint. The more you respond to his gentle pressure, the greater will be your freedom.

SIMPLE TRUTHS

The wisdom from above is first pure, then peaceable, gentle, willing to yield, full of mercy and good fruits.

JAMES 3:17

Saturday
First Week of Advent

For the Love of God

Sanctification does not depend on our geography or on our work or circumstances. Some people imagine that if they were in another place, or married to a different spouse, or had a different job, or had more money, they could do God's work so much better. The truth is that it makes no difference where they are; it all depends on whether what they are doing is God's will and done for love of him.

LIFT UP YOUR HEART

You did not choose me but I chose you.
And I appointed you to go and bear fruit,
fruit that will last.

JOHN 15:16

Sunday
Second Week of Advent

Treasures for the Soul

There must always be a relationship between the gift and the recipient—there is no point in giving anyone a treasure he cannot use. A father would not give a boy with no talent for music a Stradivarius violin. Neither will God give to egocentrics those gifts and powers and energies that they never propose to put to work in the transformation of their lives and souls.

LIFT UP YOUR HEART

Do not be conformed to this world,
but be transformed
by the renewing of your minds.

ROMANS 12:2

Monday
Second Week of Advent

Everything Is Holy

Nothing is insignificant or dull—everything can be sanctified, just as goats and sheep, fish and wheat, grapes and eyes of needles were given dignity as parables of the kingdom of God. Things the worldly wise would trample under foot become as precious to saints as pearls, for they see "sermons in stones, and good in everything" (William Shakespeare, *As You Like It*, Act II, Scene 1).

LIFT UP YOUR HEART

"See, I am laying in Zion a stone,
a cornerstone chosen and precious;
and whoever believes in him
will not be put to shame."

1 PETER 2:6

Tuesday
Second Week of Advent

Our Dignity

Every person is a precious mystery. An individual cannot be weighed by public opinion; he cannot be measured by his conditionings; he belongs to no one but himself, and no creature in all the world can penetrate his mystery except the God who made him. The dignity of every person is beyond our reckoning.

LIFT UP YOUR HEART

For it was you
who formed my inward parts;
you knit me together
in my mother's womb.

PSALM 139:13

Wednesday
Second Week of Advent

The Incarnation

Christ's coming into the world was not like that of a sightseer to a strange city, but rather like that of an artist visiting his own studio or an author paging the books he himself has written, for in becoming incarnate, the divine Word was tabernacling himself in his own creation.

IN THE FULLNESS OF TIME

Be silent, all people, before the LORD;
for he has roused himself
from his holy dwelling.

ZECHARIAH 2:13

Thursday
Second Week of Advent

Freedom of Will

God leaves each one free to reject his infusion of love—for gifts cease to be gifts if they are forced on us. God respects our freedom of will; he did not even enter into this human order of ours without consulting a woman. So neither does he elevate us to partake of his divine nature without our free consent.

LIFT UP YOUR HEART

Be pleased, O LORD, to deliver me;
O LORD, make haste to help me.

PSALM 40:13

Friday
Second Week of Advent

Acts of Virtue

Even when the will is perverse—even when a creature is enthralled and captivated by one great sinful adhesion, which makes one's days a flight from God toward lust or power—even then some few good and commendable acts contradict one's general attitude. These isolated acts of virtue are like a clean handle on a dirty bucket; with them, God can lift a soul to his peace.

LIFT UP YOUR HEART

I, the LORD,
am your Savior
and your Redeemer.

ISAIAH 60:16

Saturday
Second Week of Advent

Confession and Healing

Nothing in human experience is as efficacious in curing the memory and imagination as confession; it cleanses us of guilt, and if we follow the admonitions of our Lord, we shall put completely out of mind our confessed sins: "No one who puts a hand to the plow and looks back is fit for the kingdom of God" (Luke 9:62). Confession also heals the imagination, eliminating its anxiety for the future.

LIFT UP YOUR HEART

Purge me with hyssop,
and I shall be clean; wash me,
and I shall be whiter than snow.

PSALM 51:7

Sunday
Third Week of Advent

Faith

Faith lights up all the faculties of a person, as light inside reveals the pattern of a stained-glass window. For faith is far more than the passive acquiescence to a proof; it is a dynamic thing accompanied by an intense desire for the possession of God as the author and finisher of our life.

LIFT UP YOUR HEART

"The people who sat in darkness
have seen a great light,
and for those who sat
in the region and shadow of death
light has dawned."

MATTHEW 4:16

Monday
Third Week of Advent

Acceptance

Those who love God do not protest, whatever he may ask of them, nor doubt his kindness when he sends them difficult hours. A sick person takes medicine without asking the physician to justify its bitter taste because the patient trusts the doctor's knowledge; so the soul that has sufficient faith accepts all the events of life as gifts of God in the serene assurance that God knows best.

FROM THE ANGEL'S BLACKBOARD

*Keep yourselves in the love of God;
look forward to the mercy
of our Lord Jesus Christ
that leads to eternal life.*

JUDE 1:21

Tuesday
Third Week of Advent

The Limits of Knowledge

Intellectual knowledge is not the "one thing necessary": Not all the PhD's are saints, and all the ignorant are not demons. Indeed, a certain type of education may simply turn a man from a stupid egotist into a clever egotist and, of the two, the former has the better chance of salvation.

LIFT UP YOUR HEART

Light dawns for the righteous,
and joy for the upright in heart.

PSALM 97:11

Wednesday
Third Week of Advent

God Calls!

Sunlight is all about the house, but for sunlight to get in we must open the blinds. The physician of souls can cure, but we must know we are sick and must want to be cured. God calls! We can pretend we do not hear, we can accept him, or we can reject his voice. It is each person's inalienable right to decide.

LIFT UP YOUR HEART

Then I heard the voice of the Lord saying, "Whom shall I send, and who will go for us?" And I said, "Here am I; send me!"

ISAIAH 6:8

Thursday
Third Week of Advent

Prayer Is a Sword

Millions of favors are hanging from heaven on silken cords; prayer is the sword that will cut them. "Listen! I am standing at the door, knocking; if you hear my voice and open the door, I will come in to you and eat with you, and you with me" (Revelation 3:20).

LIFT UP YOUR HEART

Rejoice in hope,
be patient in suffering,
persevere in prayer.

ROMANS 12:12

Friday
Third Week of Advent

The Courage to Know God

It is easy to find truth; it is hard to face it, and harder still to follow it....The only people who ever arrive at a knowledge of God are those who, when the door is opened, accept that truth and shoulder the responsibilities it brings. It requires more courage than brains to learn to know God: God is the most obvious fact of human experience, but accepting him is one of the most arduous.

LIFT UP YOUR HEART

"Let us press on to know the LORD;
his appearing is as sure as the dawn;
he will come to us like the showers,
like the spring rains that water the earth."

HOSEA 6:3

Saturday
Third Week of Advent

Freedom From Sin

Prayer is dynamic, but only when we cooperate with God through surrender. The one who decides to pray for release from the slavery of carnal pleasures must be prepared, in every part of his being, to utilize the strength that God will give him and to work unreservedly for a complete freedom from sin.

LIFT UP YOUR HEART

*Create in me a clean heart,
O God, and put a new
and right spirit within me.*

PSALM 51:10

Sunday
Fourth Week of Advent

Abandonment to God

We always make the fatal mistake of thinking that it is what we do that matters, when really what matters is what we let God do to us. God sent the angel to Mary, not to ask her to do something, but to let something be done. Since God is a better artisan than you, the more you abandon yourself to him, the happier he can make you.

SEVEN WORDS OF JESUS AND MARY

O LORD, you are our Father;
we are the clay, and you are our potter;
we are all the work of your hand.

ISAIAH 64:8

Monday
Fourth Week of Advent

God's Unconditional Love

Many people nowadays want God, but on their terms, not on his. They insist that their wishes shall determine the kind of religion that is true, rather than letting God reveal his truth to them. So their dissatisfaction continues and grows. But God finds us lovable, even in our rebellion against him.

LIFT UP YOUR HEART

*I am the LORD,
I have called you in righteousness,
I have taken you by the hand
and kept you.*

ISAIAH 42:6

Tuesday
Fourth Week of Advent

The Soul's Atmosphere

Once our helplessness is rendered up to the power of God, life changes and we become less and less the victims of our moods. Instead of letting the world determine our state of mind, we determine the state of soul with which the world is to be faced. The earth carries its atmosphere with it as it revolves about the sun; so can the soul carry the atmosphere of God with it in disregard of turbulent events in the world outside.

LIFT UP YOUR HEART

I waited patiently for the LORD;
he inclined to me and heard my cry.

PSALM 40:1

Wednesday
Fourth Week of Advent

Let Go of Fear

God does not love us because we are lovable of and by ourselves, but because he has put his own love into us. He does not even wait for us to love; his own love perfects us. Letting it do this, with no resistance, no holding back for fear of what our egotism must give up, is the one way to the peace that the world can neither give nor take away.

LIFT UP YOUR HEART

There is no fear in love,
but perfect love casts out fear.

1 JOHN 4:18

Thursday
Fourth Week of Advent

God's Plan

We do not always know why such things as sickness and setbacks happen to us, for our minds are far too puny to grasp God's plan. A person is a little like a mouse in a piano, which cannot understand why it must be disturbed by someone playing Chopin and forcing it to move off the piano wires.

FROM THE ANGEL'S BLACKBOARD

*Consider him who endured such hostility
against himself from sinners,
so that you may not grow weary
or lose heart.*

HEBREWS 12:3

Friday
Fourth Week of Advent

Our Own *Fiat*

It makes no difference what you do here on earth; what matters is the love with which you do it. The street cleaner who accepts in God's name a cross arising from his state in life, such as the scorn of his peers; the mother who pronounces her *fiat* to the Divine Will as she raises a family for the kingdom of God; the afflicted in hospitals who say *fiat* to their cross of suffering are the uncanonized saints, for what is sanctity but fixation in goodness by abandonment to God's Holy Will?

SEVEN WORDS OF JESUS AND MARY

Commit your way to the LORD;
trust in him, and he will act.

PSALM 37:5

Saturday
Fourth Week of Advent

The Way to Peace

What Christ did in his own human nature in Galilee, he is doing today…in every city and hamlet of the world where souls are vivified by his Spirit. He is still being born in other Bethlehems of the world, still coming into his own and his own receiving him not, still instructing the learned doctors of the law and answering their questions, still laboring at a carpenter's bench, still "[going] about doing good" (see Acts 10:34–43), still preaching, governing, sanctifying, climbing other Calvaries, and entering into the glory of his Father.

IN THE FULLNESS OF TIME

"Glory to God in the highest heaven,
and on earth peace among those
whom he favors!"

LUKE 2:14

Also From Fulton J. Sheen

If you enjoyed *Advent Meditations With Fulton J. Sheen*, please contact us for more information about the six best-selling books quoted in this pamphlet.

Lift Up Your Heart
A Guide to Spiritual Peace
800580 • $14.95

Peace of Soul
439157 • $14.95

In the Fullness of Time
Christ-Centered Wisdom for the Third Millennium
805097• $13.95

From the Angel's Blackboard
The Best of Fulton J. Sheen
439256 • $14.95

Simple Truths
Thinking Life Through With Fulton J. Sheen
801693 • $9.95

Seven Words of Jesus and Mary
Lessons on Cana and Calvary
807084 • $9.95

Order from your local bookstore or write to
Liguori Publications
One Liguori Drive, Liguori, MO 63057-9999

Please add 15% to your total for shipping and handling.
For faster service, call toll-free 1-800-325-9521, or visit www.liguori.org
Please have your credit card handy.